MLTW
Moore, Lyndon, Turnbull & Whitaker

The Sea Ranch
Condominium 1/Moonraker Recreation Center/Ohlson Recreation Center

Residential Masterpieces 29
MLTW/Moore, Lyndon, Turnbull and Whitaker
The Sea Ranch
Condominium 1/Moonraker Recreation Center/Ohlson Recreation Center

Texts by William Turnbull, Jr. and Donlyn Lyndon
Photographs by Yukio and Yoshio Futagawa
Art direction: Gan Hosoya

Copyright © 2019 A.D.A. EDITA Tokyo Co., Ltd.
3-12-14 Sendagaya, Shibuya-ku, Tokyo 151-0051, Japan
All rights reserved. No part of this publication may be reproduced,
stored in a retrieval system, or transmitted,
in any form or by any means, electronic, mechanical,
photocopying, recording, or otherwise,
without permission in writing from the publisher.

Copyright of photographs
©2019 GA photographers

Printed and bound in Japan

ISBN 978-4-87140-562-1 C1352

Residential Masterpieces 29

MLTW
Moore, Lyndon, Turnbull & Whitaker

The Sea Ranch
Condominium 1/Moonraker Recreation Center/Ohlson Recreation Center

Sea Ranch, California, U.S.A.
1963-65/1964-66/1968-69

Texts by William Turnbull, Jr. and Donlyn Lyndon

Photographed by Yukio and Yoshio Futagawa

世界現代住宅全集29
MLTW／ムーア, リンドン, ターンブル＆ウィテカー
シーランチ
コンドミニアム 1　1963-65
ムーンレイカー・レクリエーションセンター　1964-66
オルソン・レクリエーションセンター　1968-69
アメリカ合衆国, カリフォルニア州, シーランチ

文：ウィリアム・ターンブル, ドンリン・リンドン

撮影：二川幸夫　編集・撮影：二川由夫

シーランチ──ウィリアム・ターンブル
The Sea Ranch *by William Turnbull, Jr.*

「シーランチ」はカリフォルニア沿岸，5,000エーカー（2000ヘクタール）に及ぶ開発で，サンフランシスコ湾の北，90マイル（144キロ）の所にある。長さ16キロの狭く長い地所，沢山の入江と岩の崖の海際から，土地全体に及ぶ大きな沿岸の牧草地を含み，その北端はガラーラ川が西に迂回して海に注ぐ辺りに至る。この沿岸牧草地は風よけのために海と直角に植えた糸杉が平行に並び，型通りの風景に分割される。その糸杉の区切る海岸の台地は，東側にハイウェイ1号と，樹木に覆われ数百フィート立ち上がる丘があり，素晴らしく立体的な海岸線の眺めをつくっている。

当初この土地は，レッドウッド，ビショップ・パイン，もみなどの古い木が完全な森を形成していた。だが1880年代から90年代のサンフランシスコの発展が材木を必要とし，古い森は伐採されて，海岸で不安定に錨をおろす蒸気船に積まれ出荷された。コンドミニアム（分譲共同住宅）や，レストラン・モーテルのあるブラックポイントは，1904年には材木投下用シュートとか，家，納屋，電話までついた小さなホテルのある小村として栄えていた。伐採が完了すると，伐採業とその従事者の居住地は，羊をつれた牧業に取って代わったのである。伐採のあとの切株もきれいに焼き払われ，新しい草が芽生える。シーランチ海岸は50年間に草が育てられ，糸杉が家畜保護のために植えられた。ブラックポイントは見離され，1950年代までここは絵にかいたような田園風景を保っていた。

1960年初頭，北カリフォルニア海岸の牧羊の経済性は，土地の開発といっ，別の角度から見直されるに至った。それはアルフレッド・ボークを長とするオーシャニック・プロパティーズ，キャッスル＆クック社の子会社による。ボークは，特殊な田園余暇村が，都市や郊外に仕事場を持つ人々に歓迎されるであろうチャンスを見出した。今では「シーランチ」として知られている一つの計画に翻案するため，ボークは土地の計画をローレンス・ハルプリン事務所に，主要建物の設計はジョゼフ・エシュリック事務所と，ムーア／リンドン／ターンブル／ウィテカーのMLTW事務所を考えたのである。

地理生態学者リチャード・レイノルズとともに，ハルプリンは事務所を駆って，その場所の視覚的な性格を決定する，景観の物理要因と相互作用の完全な分析をしようとした。土地の他，植物，土壌，排水，風，微気候の研究は，結果として大勢の人にこの海岸の景観を紹介する計画の進行を促進する合理的な見解となった。

現状を尊重し繁栄させようとする希望が，ハルプリンのマスタープランに盛り込まれた。それは全住民に「シーランチ」の閑静な開放性を楽しませるものであった。住居は生垣にもぐり，同様に風が決定する支配的な木立の線を用いて，建物のさまざまな形と品位とを，積極的に関連させようとした。さらに建物の間は，誰もが楽しめる公共のオープンスペースとされた。建物のセットバックは敷地の背後の土地を示すためにつくられ，公共部分の所有権は，人工のものをのさばらせない私有空間のまま保存することにされた。森の覆う丘側の道は，一見風景を邪魔しないように置かれ，敷地は眺めとプ

The *Sea Ranch* is a 5,000 acre development on the California coast, approximately 90 miles north of San Francisco Bay. It is a long narrow piece of property, 10 miles in length, running from the ocean's edge with numerous protected beaches and rocky cliffs to a large coastal meadow stretching the entire length of the Ranch and terminating on the north where the Gualala River bends westward to meet the sea. This coastal grassland is subdivided into formal landscape spaces by parallel lines of cypress hedgerows planted for windbreaks at right angles to the ocean. The coastal plateau, with its cypress walls, is enclosed on the east by Highway One and a forested ridge rising several hundreds of feet above the meadow, offering magnificent overviews up and down the coastline.

Originally the land was completely forested by old stands of redwood, Bishop pine and fir, but the development of San Francisco in the 1880's and 1890's created the demand for timber and the old forests were logged and the timber dragged down to the ocean edge to be shipped by steam schooners from precarious anchorages along the coast. Black Point, the site of the condominium and restaurant motel, was in 1904 a thriving little village with log loading chutes, houses, barns and even a small hotel complete with telephone. Upon the completion of the cutting, logging and loggers' habitations were superseded by ranchers with their bands of sheep. The cutover acreage was burned to clear the logging debris and germinate new grasses. For fifty years the Sea Ranch coast was grazed and the cypress trees were planted to shelter the livestock. Black Point was abandoned and by the 1950's Sea Ranch had evolved as a picturesque pastoral landscape.

By the early 1960's the economics of sheep ranching along the Northern California coast had become replaced by another set of economics; that of land development. Oceanic Properties, a subsidiary of Castle and Cook, under the leadership of Alfred Boeke, saw the opportunities for a special type of rural recreational community for the enjoyment of people whose working lives required urban and suburban locations. In order to translate these opportunities into what is now known as the *Sea Ranch*, Boeke retained Lawrence Halprin and Associates for land planning, and the firms of Joseph Esherick & Associates and Moore, Lyndon, Turnbull, Whitaker as architects for the initial buildings.

Halprin, with his geographer-ecologist Richard Reynolds, led his office into a thorough and complete analysis of the physical components of the landscape and their interactions which in turn determine the visual characteristics of the place. Vegetation, soil, drainage, wind and micro-climate studies coupled with topography provided a rational comprehension from which to start a planning process that would, in the end, introduce people in great numbers to this coastal landscape.

The desire to respect and enhance the existing conditions led Halprin to suggest a masterplan that would allow all residents to enjoy the quiet open character of the *Sea Ranch*. Houses were to be tucked up to the hedgerows, both for climatic protection in this cool and windy environment, as well as the utilization of the dominant tree lines to organize potentially diverse forms and tastes in building. Space between was to be common and open for the enjoyment of all. Setbacks were drawn to indicate areas on the rear of lots where houses could

ライバシーが高まるように配置された。景観の中の人工的要素が与える気分を考え，けばけばしい色の使用をやめさせ，また強く反射して目を射るような仕上げも禁止されることになった。

ハルプリンの仕事と，ボーク，エシュリック，MLTW事務所間で進行中に行われた討論により，建築の当面するデザインの諸問題を明白にし，結実させた。むき出しの土地に及ぼす太陽と風という気候条件が，建物を置くためには前提になったが，それは内部のシェルターと同じく外部をも決定することになった。冷たい海を渡ってくる北西の常風が，夏期，霧を伴う冷たい気候をもたらし，霧は日陰を不快にし，日光が歓迎されるのである。庇は思わしくなく，「風の陰」をつくることが改めてデザインの基準になった。

エシュリックの事務所は開発の一部として，第1の生垣の風上にグループとしてまとまる一戸建住居を計画した。6戸の住居は，構造と一体化した庭囲いの廻る，暖かな南面の中庭を越えて風が吹き上がるような斜めの屋根を持ち，まとめて建てられた。選ばれた外部の羽目は木製のこけら葺き，幾つかの屋根には芝生を使い，堅実にまた簡明に人工と自然景観の両者を混在させている。遠くから見ると，屋根の勾配と風の形を示す生垣とが互いに補い合い，調和のうちに全戸を一体化している。

一方，コンドミニアムはまた別の住居問題に対応した。問題への挑戦と負わされた課題は，住まう人の数が多くなり，核家族住居以上に高密化することがはっきりわかっている場合でも，その景観の性格を保存するシステムを開発することであった。この目的に向かって，ハイウェイと岩の崖との間の極めて制限された35エーカー（14ヘクタール）の沿岸地に，各戸どうしの様々なつながり方を模索していった。われわれの分析が求めたのは，露出した岩や草のある窪みといった小さなランドマークが性格づける，既存の微景観を見つけて配置することであった。ランドスケープの各要素の個性を，建物が強めたり明らかにする，またこのような場所ごとの連携を通して，それぞれにバリエーションをつくりだすことが，われわれの望みであった。グループの各戸の場所の違いや，大きさのもつ一連の目的，またそのもとになる規約は，ドンリン・リンドンが趣意書に述べる，次の要項に合うものだと思う。

「〈敷地の基準〉
どの家もこの特殊な敷地の中で識別できる個性を持たなければならない。このことは，各々が特色のある眺めを持つべきだという意味に転換できよう。西へのダイレクトな眺望，あるいは単に海の眺めが得られれば満足というわけではない。各戸は敷地から直接アクセスできること。南向きは非常に望ましい。全体の配置によりそれぞれが風よけとして機能するべきである。道は各戸のプライバシーを高めるよう木か壁で遮られるべきである。
〈建物の基準〉
室内は，その1戸が充分に一つの効果を上げるように，できるだけ開放的であるべきである。その主たる空間の中には特殊な場所をつくるべきである。

be built and ownership intermediate to the common was described as a reserve private space where no man-made structure could intrude. Roads on the forested hillside were located to minimize their visual intrusion on the landscape and lots were situated where opportunities for views and private vantages occurred. Concerns about the impact of man-made elements in landscape led to the formation of restrictions to prevent indiscriminate use of jarring colors and eye catching reflective finishes.

Halprin's work and ongoing discussions with Boeke and the Esherick and MLTW offices clarified and crystallized the design problems facing the architects. The climatic factors of sun and wind coupled with exposed topography caused a premium to be placed on buildings that would provide their own exterior as well as interior shelter. The ever present wind from the Northwest moving over cold ocean water created a cool climate with summer fogs where shade was not pleasant and sunlight was a welcome addition. Overhangs were not desirable and "wind shadows" became a newly found design criteria.

The Esherick office explored as one part of the development the opportunities for the traditional individual houses clustered together on the windward edge of the first hedge row. The houses, six in number, were grouped with shed roofs sloped to pitch wind over warmer south facing courtyards while garden walls link the structures together. The exterior siding selected was a wood shingle and the use of sod on several roofs neatly and succinctly brought together and intermingled the man-made and natural landscapes. From a distance the pitch of the roofs and the wind-shaped silhouette of the hedgerow complement each other and provide a harmoniously integrated total unit.

The condominium on the other hand was a response to a different kind of residential problem. Its challenge and task was to evolve a system for preserving the character of the landscape while housing people in higher numbers and tighter densities than single family housing is capable of achieving. To this end we explored various types of unit relationship on a severely restricted 35-acre section of coastland between the highway and the edge of the rocky cliffs. Our analysis sought to identify and locate existing micro landscapes which in turn could be characterized by their micro-landmarks such as a rocky outcrop or grassy swale. It was our intent that buildings reinforce and clarify the identity of each landscape element and through such territorial partnership create a validity for their own location. As a set of goals or ground rules for the disposition and size of each of the groups of units we felt that they should meet the following requirements as described by Donlyn Lyndon in his program notes:

Site Criteria:
All units must have 'identity' with this specific site. This can be interpreted to mean each must have a distinctive ocean view. Views directly west, or simply out to sea, should not be accepted as satisfactory. Units must have direct accessibility to site. Southern exposures are highly desirable. Arrangement of units should act as wind breaks. Road should be screened either by trees or walls where they affect the privacy of the unit.

たとえば，a) 暗い暖炉のある中心部分。b) 開放的なサンルーム（日光の入る場所），またはポーチ（気候条件によって閉鎖可能のこと）。c) 単純化した厨房と浴室の組み合わせ。d) 寝る場所（空間全体を活用する）。明かり取りの開口部は，目を見張る眺めの効果を上げるために，また大きな内部空間を感じさせるつもりで配置すべきである。大きな倉庫は，狭くなりがちな各戸の面積を減らさないように，車庫に置くこと。

〈一般的な推奨事項〉
自然の土地の形や尺度を強調する態度で各戸を配置すべきである。道路システムを単純化し，外から直接入る各戸の機能を満たし，しかもグループとして積極的な統一感を盛り上げるため，車はまとめて庭の一部に置くこと。部分を加え合わすよりも，大きなスケールの複合体をつくりあげるため，各戸を集めて効果を出すべきである。材料は素材のまま，単純にすべきであり，この単純さと便利さは，同様に厨房や浴室に当てるべきである。その数からして，各戸は敷地の上に大きく，建築的にはひとまとめになろう。長所としてこの点をとりあげるべきである。風景と同化するように隠されたり，つくられたりすべきではない。」

『ワールド・アーキテクチュア2』より抜粋

このような規約で仕事を進め，われわれは10から20の住居をグループにして敷地のマスタープランに取り組んだ。最初に10戸が展示用のモデルハウスとして選ばれ，その敷地はエシュリックの設計した店舗と，土地会社の販売事務所に近い所に選ばれた。敷地自体は草の生えた吹きさらしの台地（原始的な岩礁の名残りを留める）で，眼下で荒波が岩を嚙んだ切り立った崖に近い所であった。雰囲気をもった不毛な感じの，素晴らしい場所であった。

この敷地にわれわれは，24フィート（7.3メートル）の立方体の建物10戸を配置した。各戸は眺めを主にして置かれ，外部の生活空間を保護するように考慮した。各戸は敷地勾配に沿う，1枚の大きな屋根の下に集められた。その屋根が全体をひとまとめにし，ランドスケープの大きさに呼応する全体の尺度となったのである。

24フィート（7.3メートル）の立方体の中で，いつでも太陽の暖かさを引き込む沢山のスカイライト以外には窓を少なくして，内部に保護されているという，囲われた感覚を最大に生かそうとした。立方体の外側は，窓の部分，テラス，デッキ，そして囲まれた庭，風に対抗して囲いをとることになったとしても，内よりも外のことを考えた。つながりとしては，眺めの特質や土地との関係と同様に，また空間全体の原則と構造を加味しながら，それぞれがバリエーション豊かに個性を持てるように計画されたのである。

構造システムは，重い木材で形をつくり，10インチ×10インチ（25センチ角）の柱と，4インチ×10インチ（10センチ×25センチ）の梁材で構成した。また4インチ×4インチ（10センチ×10センチ）の斜め材との剛接合の部分には直径3フィート（914センチ）の鉄の円板の一片が用いられている。柱は最少数になる

Building Criteria:
Interior spaces should be kept open to create the effect of as generous a unit as possible. Within general space there should be specific places created for: (a) A dark fire place center. (b) An open solarium/porch. (capable of being closed off in inclement weather). (c) Simplified kitchen-bath combination. (d) Sleeping areas (taking advantage of the entire space). Light openings should be placed for striking view effects and in such a manner to create the sensation of large interior space. Large dead storage areas should be placed in carports to avoid reducing already small unit square footage.

General Recommendations:
Units should be sited in a manner reinforcing the natural land forms and scale. Cars should be grouped in courts to simplify road structure, maintain a workable unit adjacent to the ground, and be a positive unifying feature for the clusters. Units should work together making a large-scale composition that is more than an addition of pieces. Materials should be rough and simple and this attitude of simplicity and convenience applies as well to kitchen and bath. Units, by their number, will bulk large and architectural on the site and advantage should be taken of this fact. They should not be hidden or made to merge into the landscape.

—World Architecture 2, John Donat, editor

Working from such a set of rules, we evolved a masterplan for the acreage with clusters of between 10 and 20 units. An initial grouping of 10 units was chosen as a demonstration model and a specific site was selected for its proximity to the Esherick store and sales office. The site itself was a grassy windswept mound (the remnant of a prehistoric reef) adjacent to the rocky cliffs with the surf pounding below; a moody, barren and magnificent place.

On this site we set out to arrange our 10 units using a building cube of 24′. Each unit was located initially for views and then adjusted to create protected outdoor living spaces. The individual units are collected under the single large roof which follows the slope of the site. The roof acts as an organizer and creates a scale for the whole that is related to the larger scale of the landscape.

Inside the 24′ cubes we tried for a maximum sense of enclosure, of being inside and protected, with few openings except for the numerous skylights which admit the always welcome warmth of the sun. Outside the cubes went glass bays, terraces, decks and walled gardens, more outside than in, even when they are enclosed against the wind. Conditions of linkage or connection as well as idiosyncrasies of view or relationship to the grade allowed opportunities for each unit to be varied and have its own personality while at the same time partaking of the spatial discipline and structural organization of the whole.

The structural system evolved as a heavy timber frame comprised of 10″ x 10″ columns and 4″ x 10″ horizontal girt members. These were cross-braced with 4″ x 4″ and rigid connections were achieved by using segments cut from a circular three foot metal disc. Column positions were located to minimize the number required and girts set one upon another in a layered and lapped fashion. All the heavy timber was left rough sawn as it came from the mill saws and the rough texture and

ように配置され，桁は重ねる方法をとった。重い材木は全部，製材所から来たままの挽き放しで，その荒い肌ざわりと直接的な感じの構造は，敷地の生のままの野性味に精神的には合うと思われた。重い構造材の上に載る荒削りの羽目は釘打ちされて，大きな農家の納屋のように内部を仕上げ，そのレッドウッドの板が外部のたて羽目ともなっている。

各戸の寝室はできるだけ開放的で大きく見せるようにした。その結果，余暇のための場所は人が働く家とは異なり，特殊な場所であるという目的に向いた。われわれは，昔ながらの部屋の代わりにスーパー・スケールの家具を用いる計画を進めた。寝る場所は1層分の高さのある，4本の脚を持ったベッドとなり，その脚は暗い居心地の良い暖炉空間を覆う。厨房と浴室は2階建のキャビネットの中に納まり，この機能的な家具が脱衣の場所としてくりぬかれたり，倉庫になり，屋根の勾配によって高さが取れれば寝る場所を追加した。眠りのプライバシーは，視覚的には大きなキャンバスのテントでまかない，同時にスカイライトからの太陽光線を受け内部の暖かさを増すという二重の役を与えている。家具類は空間を囲う木の荒さと異なり，滑らかな木でつくられ，その家具はさらにその性質を強調するために明るい色で塗られた。各戸のつながりによって，エクストラ・ルームや，ポーチ，外部デッキができた。

所有者である開発業者は，自分の販売市場が確かではなかったために，ある住居の2階の空間の中の寝室を2部屋に分けて従来の家のように直した。だが厨房と浴室を一体化した大家具は，構造のシステムや材料と同じく元案の通りにつくられた。

車は，悪天候から守るため簡単な屋根をかけた囲われた外のスペースに集められた。地方材としてのレッドウッドが全般に用いられ，天候条件からしても特に遠くから眺めると，その構成は巨大な木造の岩のような，土着で，永遠の田園風景の中の永遠といえる性格を帯びて見える。

コンドミニアムが完成し，また土地売却の区切りもあって，「シーランチ」は成功に沸いたが，レクリエーション施設が必要となっていた。われわれはローレンス・ハルプリンとともに，先住者たちのために小さな水泳プールとテニスコートを計画するよう命じられた。敷地は2番目の生垣の真東，排水用の窪みであった。1ヶ所盛り上がった土地が，幾分か囲いをつくり「場所」としての感じはあった。だがその上を覆う建物をつくることは最高に困難であった。

問題は三つあった。第1に小さく経済的な施設で，風景を眺め，かつ損わぬものをデザインすること。第2にプールとテニスコートを，身を切るように強い北風から守ること。第3は人気を得るためにプールサイドに暖かな感じの屋外の空間をつくること。これらの解決には，プールとテニスコートを含んだ土地そのものを，風よけ用の窪みに変えることであった。プールの北側に，2層分の仕上げなしのレッドウッド壁を控え壁とともに立て，「風よけ用のダム」と陽射しの反射用に働かせたのである。控え壁の間は，レッドウッドのこけら葺き屋根や半透明プラスチック屋根で覆い，ロッカー室，シャ

the straightforward expression of the structure seemed psychologically appropriate for the raw and wild qualities of the site. Onto the heavy timber frame rough sawn vertical boards were nailed completing the big barnlike interiors and providing a surface for the exterior vertical redwood boards.

For the interiors of the units we were desirous of keeping the space as open and seemingly as large as possible. To this end and toward the goal that a vacation place is special and different from one's work-a-day abode, we developed a scheme that used super-scaled furniture pieces in lieu of traditional rooms. A sleeping place became a four-poster bed, itself a story high, and sheltering underneath its legs a dark cozy fireplace area. The kitchen and bath became a stacked two-story cabinet and this functional bureau was hollowed out for dressing places and storage as well as additional sleeping spaces when grade and roof height allowed. Privacy for the sleeping was provided visually by huge canvas tents which, when down, did a double service on catching the sun from the sky lights and providing a warm glow for the interior of the unit. The furniture pieces are constructed of smooth wood to set them apart from the rough spatial enclosure and painted in bright colors to further emphasize their furniture characteristics. Linkages created extra special rooms, porches and outside decks.

Because the owner-developer was unsure of his market, some of the units were more traditionally handled with upstairs loft sleeping areas divided into two bedrooms. The kitchen-bath cabinet was maintained as well as the structural system and materials.

On the exterior cars are collected in a walled compound under simple sheds for weather protection. Local materials, in this case redwood, are used throughout and the composition, as it weathers, especially at a distance, takes on all the characteristics of a great wooden rock, indigenous and timeless in the timeless rural landscape.

With the completion of the condominium and the commencement of land sales the *Sea Ranch* enjoyed a success that led to the need for organized recreational facilities. We were asked at this point, in conjunction with Lawrence Halprin, to provide a small swimming pool and tennis court for these new pioneer residents. The site was a drainage swale just east of the second hedgerow. A fold in the land provided some shelter and a sense of "place" but maximized subsurface construction difficulties.

The problem was a triple one: first, to design a small and inexpensive facility that would be part of the sweep of the landscape and not an interruption of it; second, to shield the swimming pool and the tennis court from the brisk, strong north wind; and third, to create the sensation of warmth necessary to make the outdoors alongside a swimming pool an attractive idea. The solution evolved with a reshaping of the land itself into wind-free pockets containing the swimming pool and tennis court. On the north side of the pool a two-story unfinished redwood wall with attendant buttresses serves as "wind dam" and sun reflector. Spaces between buttresses when enclosed and covered with redwood shingles or translucent plastic roofs form locker rooms, showers and saunas for men and women, with their adjacent storage areas. Interiors have been painted by Barbara Stauffacher Solomon with multi-col-

*Coastline of West Coast:
View from Highway 1 leading to the Sea Ranch, 2019*

Gate of the Sea Ranch, 1970

ワー，サウナなどを男女別に，付属する倉庫と合わせてつくった。室内はバーバラ・スタウファカー・ソロモンが，白い合板の壁の上に多色のグラフィックパターンを描いた。それは鮮明で，超スケールなものとなり，外部の静かさ，静隠な草地と対を成すものになった。低い杉がハイウェイを隠すために道沿いの草地に植えられ，東に向かう森の坂道を延長する形となった。

公共部分に興味が向けられる一方，組織化された販売活動が敷地販売を増加させていた。開発会社の中での開発と経済条件への圧力が，高密度化の敷地配置をはかる当初のハルプリンの計画案を避けるようになっていった。「シーランチ」に人が来るほど，もっと家が建てられるほどに別のレクリエーション施設が求められた。古い馬小屋からは乗馬が考えられ，また夏期の水泳と水浴びのためには，ランチの東の丘の背後を流れるガララ川に下りる道がつくられた。同時に最初のテニスコートやプールへは，人々が押しかけて過剰となり，1968年には第2のレクリエーション施設の計画に声がかかった。

この新しい施設は，納屋に近い糸杉の生垣のすぐ南，プール周辺に風が当たらないように配置された。構造は第1の場合より複雑で，テニスコートの風よけにもなるように，プールの南側に置かれた。この場合の中心壁は，二つの半透明な屋根付きの廊下に対して，背骨のように働いている。全体は三つの塔で貫かれ，中央は男子用のサンルーム，続いてベンチの置かれた女子用屋外サウナ，そして自立する塔はプールの目印となり，海岸に至る下の歩行路の視線の一端となっている。ロッカー室には利用者用入口からある決まったシークエンスで空間がつながっている。水着，テニス着に着替える場所，下って外に出る。帰る時はこの逆の順序，シャワーから着替え。サウナは男女別と家族用に分かれ，外部を眺める窓がある。室内に水の落ちる所があり，その大きさ，明るい色彩，陽光に溢れた空間が，昔の浴場を思い起こさせる。

外のテニスコートは，さらに風を除けるために大地を掘って沈み，その土手も遮蔽に使われている。日光浴のための木造の「隆起物」がプールに接して置かれているが，その塔は機械室として使われ，同時に子供たちのための滑り台である。プールの中の島は正式の25メートルコースと，遊び用プールを分けている。

「シーランチ」にはこのように沢山の特殊な場所がある。ここを訪れた人の心に残るのは，体験の集積であり，特殊な地理であり，昔の田園を伝える草と糸杉の風景の展開である。風景といい建築といい，成長，変化，結果と絶えず進む過程の中で，思想を表現するものである。

1970年執筆
（和訳：三沢浩）

ored patterns of graphic overlay on white plywood walls, which produce a vivid, overscaled counterpart to the quiet, serene grass forms of the exterior. Seedling pines were planted in the natural grasses along the highway to screen it and form an extension of the forested slopes to the east.

Continuing interest on the part of the public coupled with a well organized selling campaign led to more lot sales. Pressure for development and economic conditions within the developing company led to relinquishing of the earlier Halprin planning ideals regarding density and lot arrangement. As more people came to the Ranch and built more houses, other recreational facilities were required. Horseback riding was introduced from the old stables and a road was cut down to the Gualala River behind the eastern ridge of the Ranch for summer swimming and splashing. Eventually the pressure on the first tennis court and swimming pool became excessive, and in 1968 plans went ahead for a second recreational facility.

The new facility is situated just south of the cypress hedgerow adjacent to the stable-barn and located to provide a wind-free condition for the pool area. The structure, a more complex version of its predecessor, was placed south of the pool in a position to provide a wind shadow for the tennis courts. The central wall in this case acts as a spine against which two translucent roofed corridors are nestled. The whole is punctuated by three towers; a central one for men's sunbathing, an attached exedra form to celebrate the ladies' outdoor sauna slide and a free standing element that marks the pool and terminates the vista of the sunken walkway to the beach. The locker room are a series of spaces experienced in orderly sequential process of public entrance, private changing to swimming or tennis clothes, thence lower exit, and then later the reverse procedure of shower and change. Saunas are provided for each sex as well as a family unit with windows for exterior views. Interior cold water plunges are provided and the grand, brightly painted and sunfilled spaces recall the "baths" of another era.

On the exterior the tennis courts are dug into the landscape for additional wind protection and berms are further used to screen them. A wooden "reef" for sunbathing lies adjacent to the pool and its tower, while functionally acting as a place for the mechanical equipment, also containing a water slide for children of all ages. An island in the pool divides the 25-meter olympic area from the less serious minded efforts.

The *Sea Ranch* is, in the end, many such special places. It is memorable to the participant as a collection of experiences, a special geography, an evolution from the grass and cypress landscape of a previous rural generation. Both the landscape and the architecture represent ideas in the ever ongoing processes of growth, change and fruition.

Written in 1970

Condominium 1 1963-65

Condominium 1 consists of 10 units with 24-feet (7.3-meter) cubic modules, 1968

View from southeast. Exterior redwood walls are renewed for each unit, 2019

Southwest elevation with roof pitched at 15 degrees, 2019

Location

Site plan

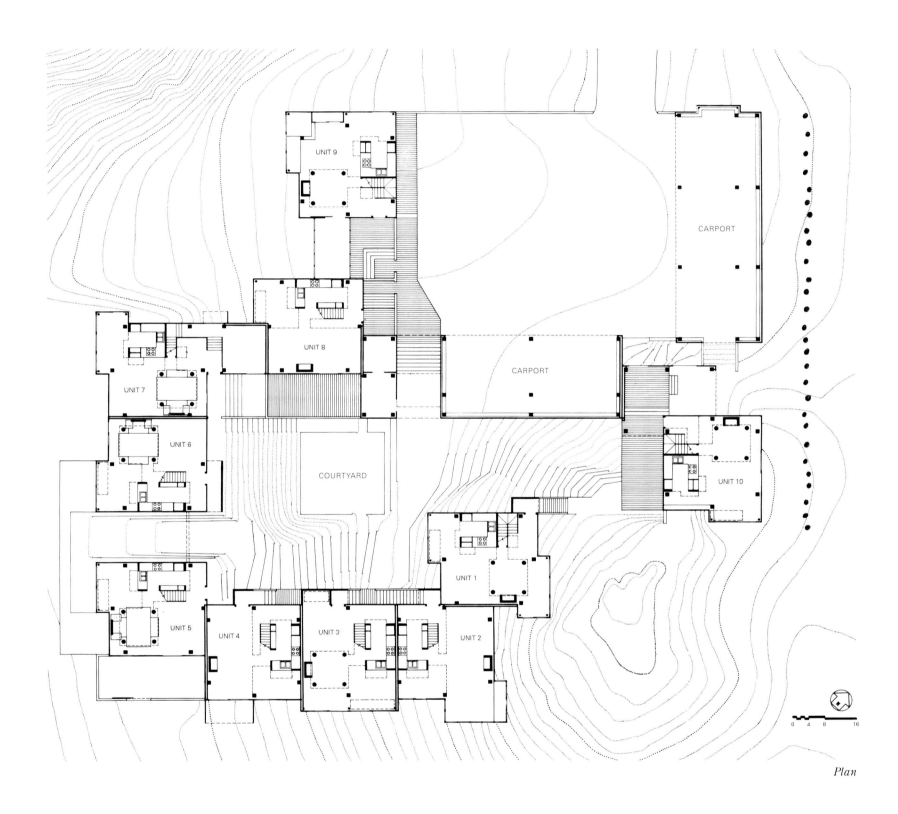

Plan

View from approach on northeast, 1970

*View toward courtyard from upper point.
Unit 1 (originally Lyndon's house) on left, 1968*

Courtyard, 2019

Courtyard Left leading to unit B, 2019

Courtyard. View from lower point, 1970

Sunroom of unit 2, 1968

View toward unit 10, 2019

Kitchen on first floor

Bathroom on second floor

Plan detail of kitchen and bathroom/Type B (unit 9)

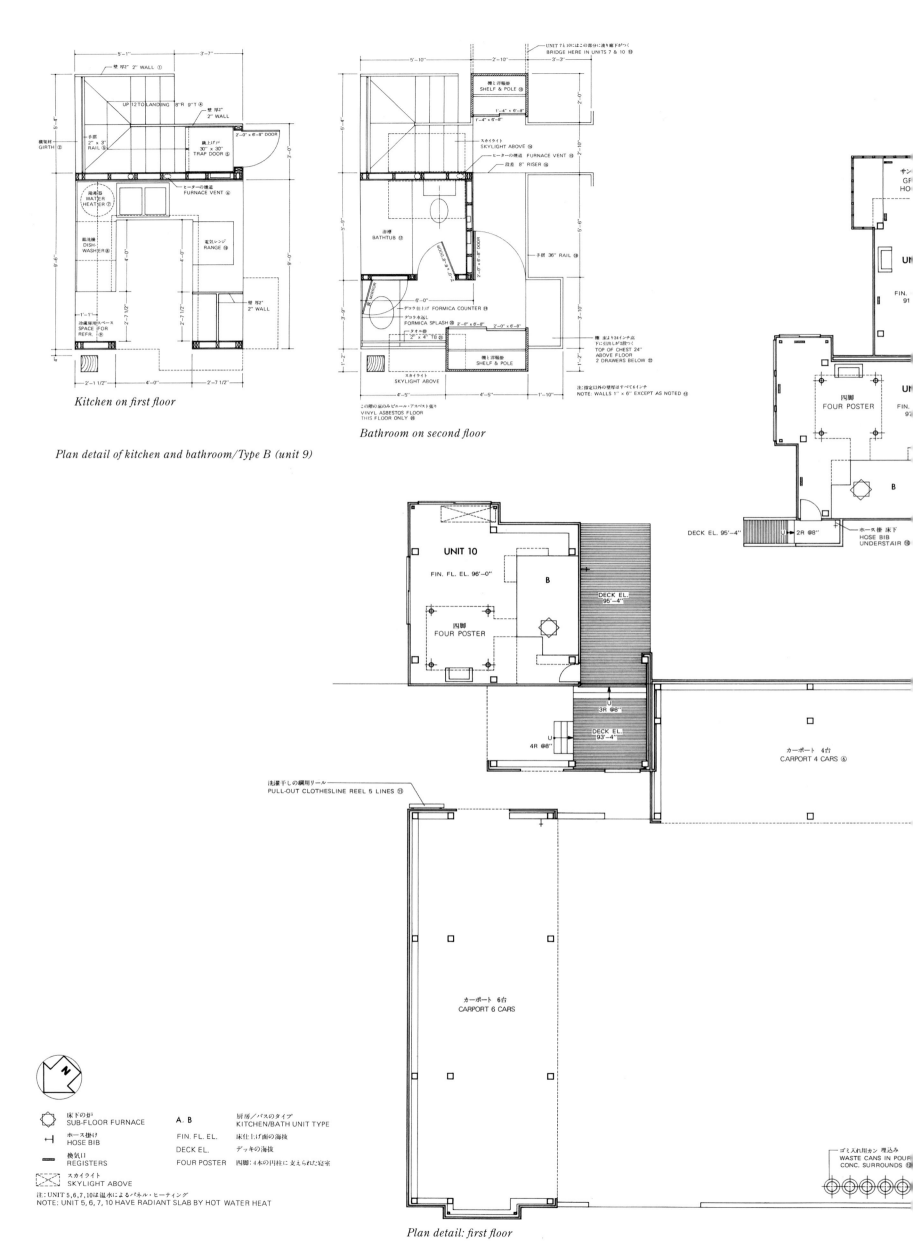

Plan detail: first floor

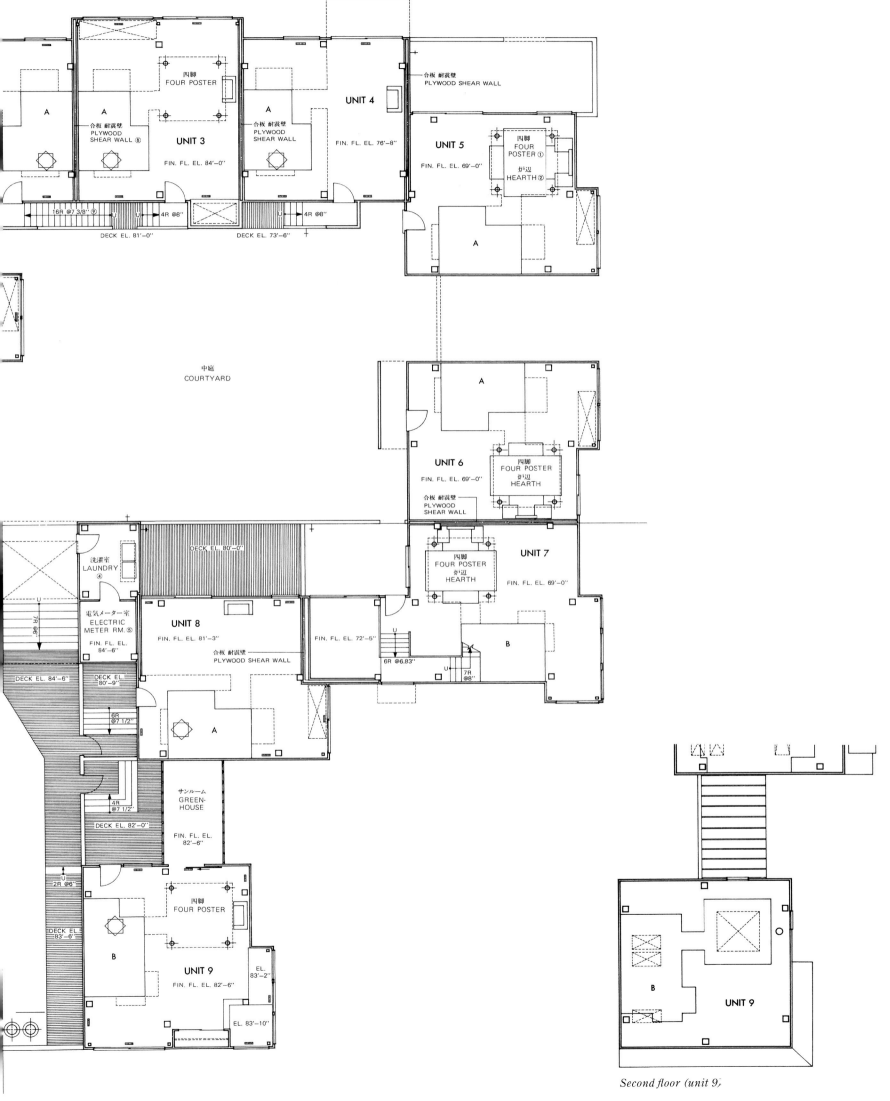

Second floor (unit 9)

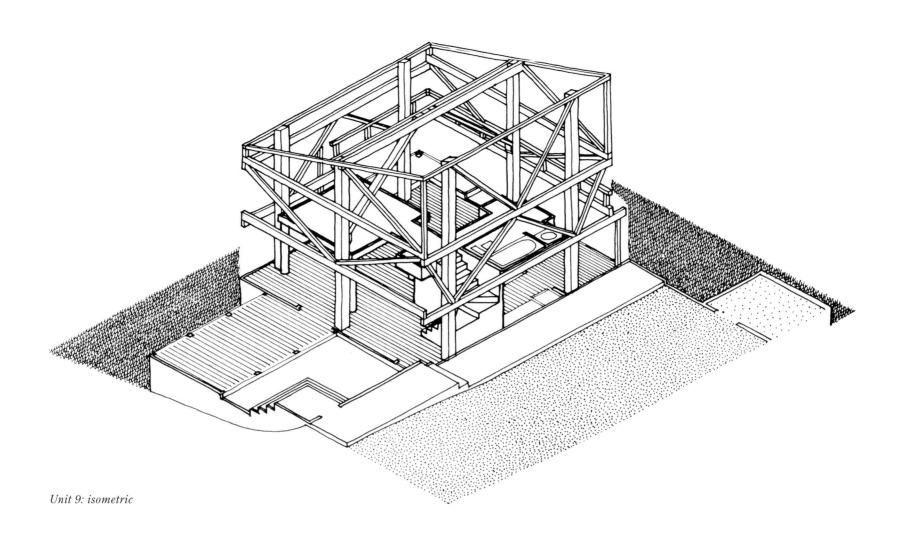

Unit 9: isometric

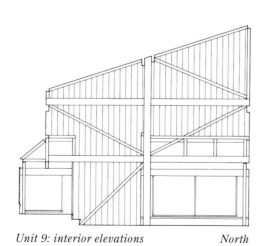
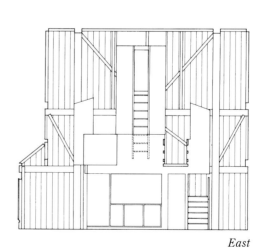

Unit 9: interior elevations   North   East

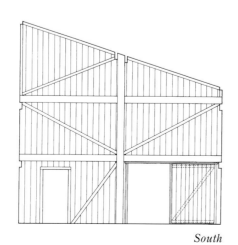
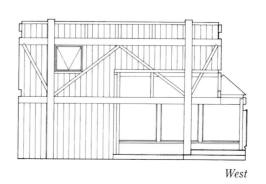

South   West

Pathway to courtyard from carport

Entrance porch of unit 9

View from carport toward unit 9 (right) and unit 8 (left)

Unit 9 (Moore's house): sunroom, 1968

Unit 9 (Moore's house): living room, 2019

Unit 9 (Moore's house): two-story cabinet of kitchen and bathroom with poping-out storage and shelf, 1968

*Living room, 2019. Raised four-poster bed ("Aedicule") for sleeping place above.
Sunroom inmost was converted into bedroom later by Moore*

Unit 9 (Moore's house): bay window with view of Pacific Ocean, 2019

Fireplace, 2019. Unit 9 is decorated with Moore's vast collection of toys

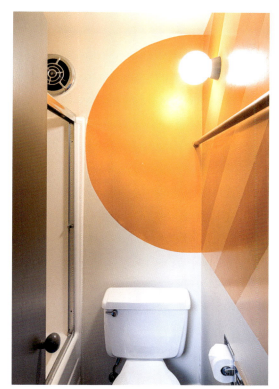

Bathroom with supergraphics, 2019

Staircase, 2019

Staircase. Entrance on right, 2019

Unit 9 (Moore's house): second floor. Sleeping space on right, bathroom cabinet on center, 2019

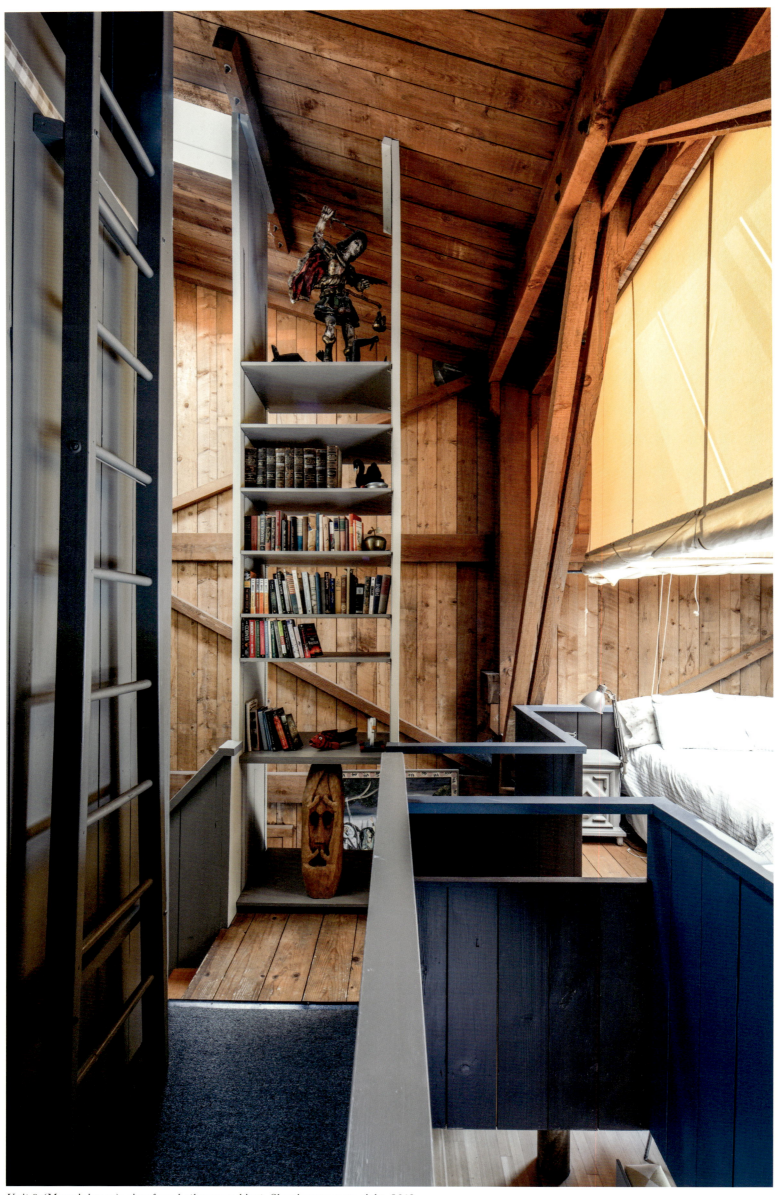

Unit 9 (Moore's house): view from bathroom cabinet. Sleeping space on right, 2019

Sleeping space, 1968

Unit 9 (Moore's house): downward view of living room, 1968

Unit 1 (originally Lyndon's house): view toward Pacific Ocean over courtyard, 1968

View toward Pacific Ocean from Condominium 1

Originally Athletic Club #1, 1968

Overall view of pool, 2019. Drainage swale was reshaped into wind-free pockets

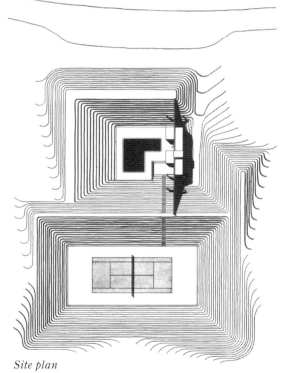

Site plan

1 WOMEN'S ENTRY
2 WOMEN'S SAUNA
3 DECK
4 MECHANICAL ROOM
5 MEN'S ENTRY
6 STORAGE
7 SHOWER ROOM
8 MEN'S LOCKER ROOM
9 WOMEN'S LOCKER ROOM
10 CHANGING
11 MEN'S SAUNA
12 MEN'S SUNDECK

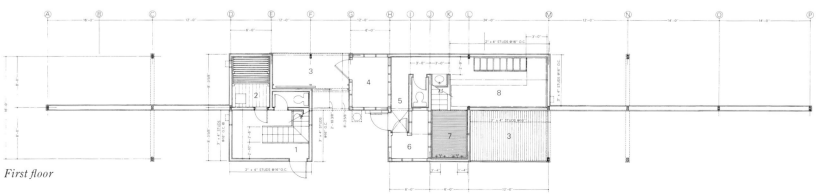

First floor

Building situated at north side of pool and walls with buttresses acting as windbreak, 1968

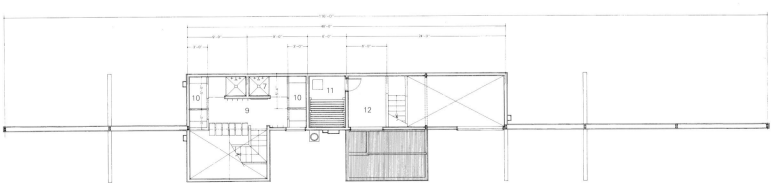

Second floor

59

Men's locker room. Supergraphics by Barbara Stauffacher Solomon, 1968

Men's locker room, 1968

Women's locker room: entry, 1968

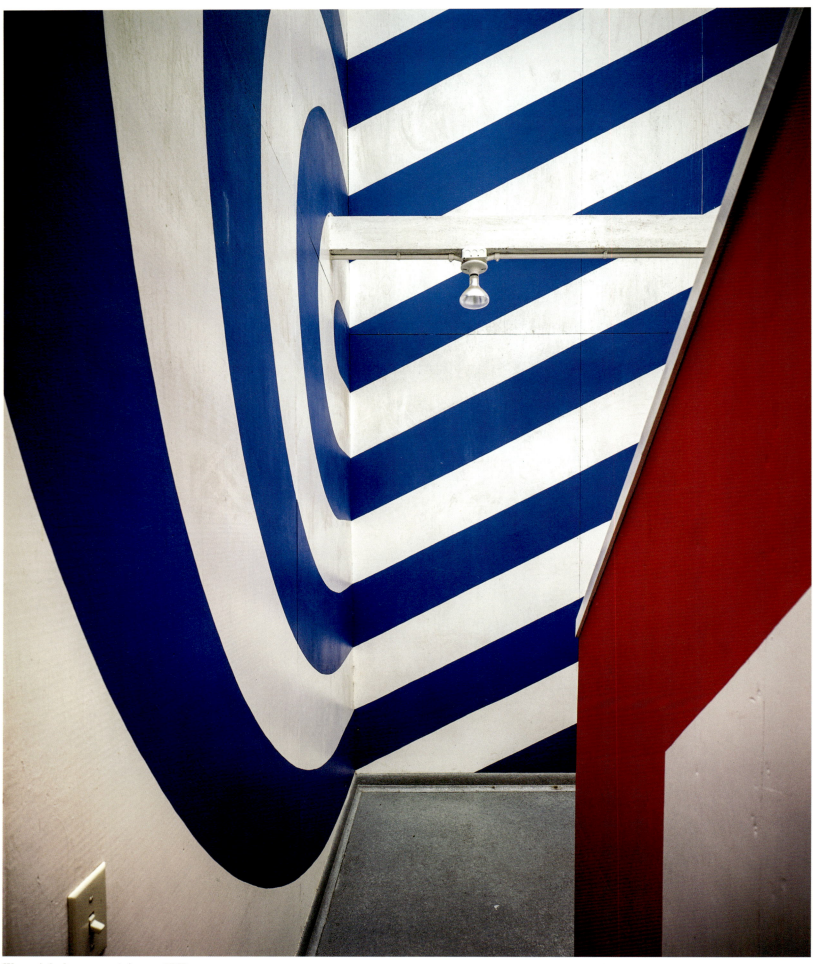
Women's locker room: staircase, 1968

*Women's locker room was renovated and its graphic patterns were covered over in 1975.
In 2018 Stauffacher Solomon restored with new graphic pattern, 2019*

Ohlson Recreation Center
1968-69

Originally Athletic Club #2, 1970

View toward Pacific Ocean, 1970

Water chute on center. Locker rooms on right, 2019

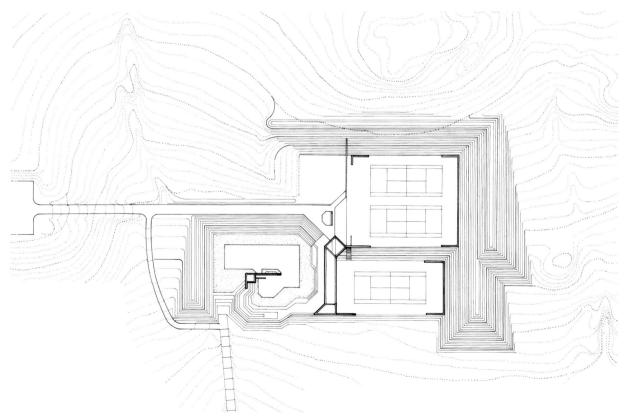

Site plan

1 PLUNGE POOL
2 WOMEN'S SUNDECK
3 STORAGE
4 MECHANICAL ROOM
5 PASSAGE
6 FAMILY SAUNA
7 MEN'S SAUNA
8 MEN'S SHOWER ROOM
9 WOMEN'S SAUNA
10 WOMEN'S SHOWER ROOM
11 WOMEN'S LOCKER ROOM
12 WOMEN'S ENTRY
13 MEN'S ENTRY
14 MEN'S LOCKER ROOM
15 DECK

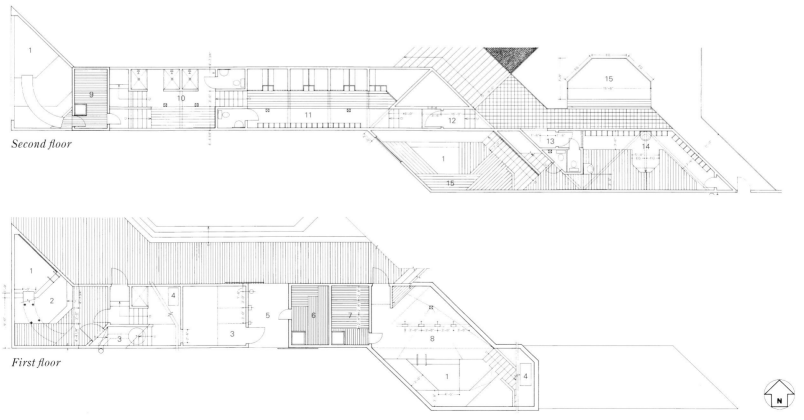

Second floor

First floor

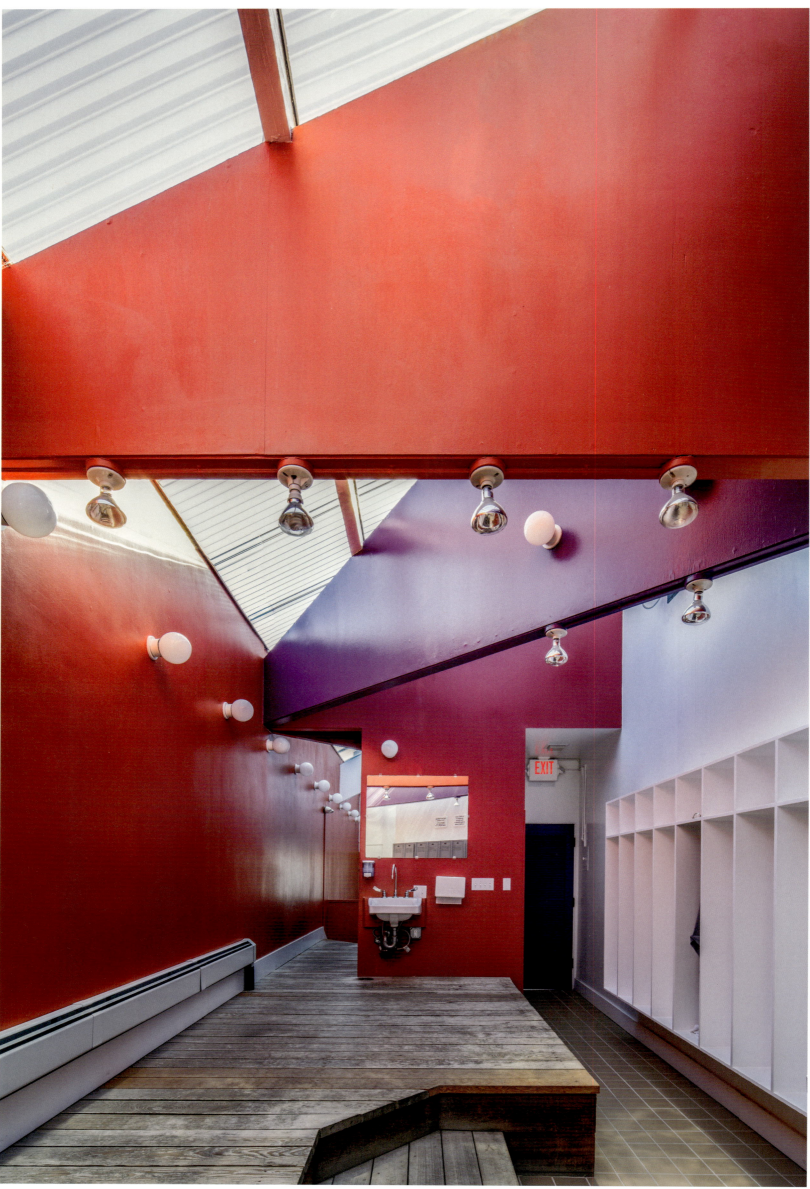

Men's locker room, 2019

Men's locker room. View from staircase to shower room below, 1970

心の宿る住まい：MLTWの住宅について——ドンリン・リンドン
The House of the Mind: Houses by MLTW *by Donlyn Lyndon*

MLTWの建築作品，あるいはその影響を受けた建築の中心となる考え方について簡単にいえば，「心の宿る住まい」のエッセンスとは，私たちが建築をつくるその場所そのもののうちに初めから存在している，ということである。私たちの設計する住宅は，その敷地にとって，それを建て，そして，そこに住まう人々にとって何か特別で，他に類のないものでありたいと願っている。もちろん，その他にも目標はあるが。建築家が敷地を活かす方法や，建築する工法とは「家」というものが根ざしているその文化的背景と深く関わり合ってでき上がっている。「心の宿る住まい」とは，一人ひとりの人にとって，その人の個人的な思い出や，あるいは反対に全く一般的にその時代のつくり出した文化の典型や，そういった諸々の事柄が複雑に織りなしてつくり上げられた複合体である。だから，建築家のなすべきことは，これらの絡まり合った複合物を内包できるような建築をつくることであり，そして，その建築の中にそれらが生き生きと展開するような建築をつくる方法を探し出すことである。

建築というものは，私たちの知る限り，人間の観念や行為をそこに集中させるためにつくる仕掛けであると言ってもよく，つまり全く規則性のない出来事の流れを相互に結び合わせ，目的を与え，そうして，その形態と，その場所特有の性格とを結び合わせることである。「家」とは入念に仕上げられた鏡であり，それはその家の構成や，その室内に置かれた調度品といったものと，その所有者が共に生活していくそのやり方を映し出すのである。またその鏡は同時に，その家の周囲の自然環境やそこに住む人々の昔の思い出をも映し出すものである。

建築の基本的な営み——床をつくり，囲いをし，屋根を掛ける——は，何らかの意味で自然を服従させ，手のうちに納めさせようとする目的を持っている。それはその上を歩けるように土地を平らにならし，風や太陽を遮り，降る雨を受けて土地に流す，といったような行為である。そしてその場合に応じてそれぞれ異なった条件に適うように，あるいは自然の変化に順応できるように，建築の形が与えられることで，自然の豊かさがその上に映し出されることも可能となる。太陽が東から西に移動するにつれて光線の具合が変わり，土地の緩やかな勾配に合わせて床やテラスが段々に変化し，屋根が，あるいは風を防いで低く構え，あるいは太陽を迎えようとして高く構えたりするのもそうした表われである。それらは私たちが建築を建てるこの自然環境を活かしたものであると言うことができる。「家」というこの鏡にはさらに，その家の壁に縁取られた窓から見える遠い風景や，近くの樹々の枝や，室内が外へ延長したとも考えられる手入れの行き届いた庭などが，さながら万華鏡のように変化して映し出されることであろう。

「心の宿る住まい」とは，だから単独に周囲と切り離されて，それだけで価値があるといったようなものではなく，毎日の日常生活の中での生活の方向づけや，動機づけをつくり出すものとして作用する時にその意味が重要になってくる。

私たちの設計のプロセスは，いくつかの建築のパターンを設計に求められた条件に沿って当てはめてみて，それが要求された条件を満たすかどうかを検討しながら，徐々にそれらを密なものにしていくことである。しかし要求とパターンの両者が必ずしも一致しなければならないということはない。あれこれとやっていくにつれて，初めの形のイメージが，これが正しいのだと，いよいよ揺るがないものになっていく場合もあるし，あるいは反対にその持っている矛盾がさらけだされることによって，これでよいのだとされる場合もある。つまり，つくり出される秩序とは柔軟性に富んでいて，解が多様に産まれるようなものが望ましいのである。

初めに無理して当てはめてみられるこうした住宅のパターンは，そこでの生活行為に直接結びつけられたものである。ふつうそれは小さな家であり，上には屋根が掛かりその下には床が何層かあり，広間には家

The work of MLTW and its descendants stems from a shared belief that the House of the Mind should be embodied in the places that we build. The houses that we design are meant to be specific, unique to the sites they are in and the people who build and occupy them; yet, more than that. The present circumstances of land, use and building technique are set in the context of culturally rooted concepts of House. The House of the Mind is for each person a complex interweaving of personal reminiscences and cultural prototype. The architect's task is to find a way of building that brings forth these associations and makes them present in the life of the building.

Architecture, as we see it, is a setting for the meeting of idea and circumstance, for giving coherence and purpose to the arbitrary flow of events, and for investing generic forms with the particular conditions of place, A house is an elaborate mirror, reflecting its owner's commitments in the way it is structured and in the things that it holds. It should reflect, as well, the complexity of nature and the fact of historical antecedents.

The basic acts of building—floor, enclosure and cover—are all acts that in some measure subject nature: making the land flat to walk on or closing off the wind and sun, or casting the rain aside. They can also reflect the bounty of nature by being shaped specifically, responding to the different conditions that they meet or revealing the presence of natural variation: light changing as the day changes, floors and terraces stepped gradually as the land is, a roof sloped low to the wind or high to the sun. These are all qualities that tally with the natural world in which we build. To these reflections may be added a kaleidoscope of changing views framed by the walls of a house; opening where possible to far views of the surrounding landscape, close views of the branches of a tree or the cultivated near ground that is itself an extension of the house.

The House of the Mind, then becomes important not as an independent scheme valuable in itself, but as a compelling source of direction and motivation when working with the specifics of everyday life.

Our design process begins with imposing one of a few archetypal patterns into the stated needs of a program, then elaborating the implications of that choice to see how well it can fit. Congruence is not necessarily the aim. With proper juggling the initial formal idea can be confirmed as much by contradiction as by reinforcement, Revealing the fragility of order and the fecundity of circumstance is, we think, appropriate.

The archetypal schemes so imposed are ones that relate directly to acts of habitation: the little house, with roof revealed above and a stepped floor below, the great hall, which is occupied by giant elements of furniture, the passage or atrium that flows into rooms on either side.

The purpose of this first pattern is to estab-

具が所狭しと置かれ，部屋の片側は廊下になり，もう片方は中庭に面している。

この最初のパターンは，住宅の中のさまざまの意味を持ったそれぞれの場所にそれぞれの位置を与え，さらに住宅の総ての部分が関係しなければならない外部空間の位置を決め，それらの構成の最初の公式をつくり出す働きをする。このパターンを決めるのにはいろいろのやり方がある。例えば中心点を決めて，そこからその家の隅々にまでその秩序が行き渡っていくものや（ジョブソン邸やジョンソン邸にそれは見られる），ぐるりと周囲を取り囲む壁を強く浮き出させて内部空間の一体性を強めるものや（ニューヘヴンのムーア自邸やオークランドのタルバート邸に見られる），内外の境目に特別の意味を与える，例えば広大な外部空間の広がりに面していたり（オットセン邸やチャムピイ邸），廊下に面して部屋を並べたりする（ラッシュ邸やスターン邸），あるいはその両方の性格を持っている家（ハインズ邸）などが挙げられる。時には異なったパターンの組み合わせが，いくつかの異なったスケールの並列の面白さをつくり出すこともある（シーランチ・コンドミニアムやオリンダのムーア自邸）。

これらのパターンを建築要素の構成のダイアグラムに置き換えていくのはそれほど難しいことではない。その時に，柱列や，箱や，対になった壁やコロネードなどが有効に働く。こうして建築要素の組み合わせができ上がると，残りのデザインプロセスとは，この基本的な形をあれこれ想像を働かせながら周囲の環境にあてはめてみるということになる。場所を活かして使うということは，一方では建築をランドスケープの中に定着させ，一方では空間相互が外部空間と持つ関係について考えることである。それは，腰を下ろす場所であったり，リスのやって来る場所であったり，友達と集ったり，柱に寄りかかったり，壁にもたれて休んだりする場所であったりする。建築の構成された要素の後ろに，上に，下に，前に，そして並んでつくられた室内と屋外との境の空間について想を練ることである。

そして，こうした筋立てが展開するにつれて，次に建築の諸々のより細かな要素，差し掛けや，張り出し窓や，ポーチや，そういった特別の機能を充たし，室内と屋外の境目の部分の印象を生活的にする要素が付け加えられていく。さらにヴォイドな空間も付け加えられ，──中庭や，ニッチや，その他建築に引っ込みの部分がつくられて，光を特別のところに招き入れたり，外壁に庇のついた窪んだ場所を与えたりする。

壁が大変に分厚かったり，光をあまりに遮ってしまう場合には，そこには窓やドアのサイズを持った開口部が開けられたり，トラスの隙間に開口が設けられたりする。こうしてでき上がった家の形は，内と外の，さらに人間のアイディアと自然の環境との，二つの相反するものの相互の闘争的関係に関する物語風の記録となるのである。

時には，初めのパターンのスケールが大きすぎて一軒の家の中の人々の行為がすぐに満足されてしまい，何の用もない空間が余ってしまう時がある。その時にはエディキュラ（小神殿）の機能がよくそれを助けるのだが，スケールを落としてくることによって，空間に焦点を与えることが有効である。その場合，必ずしもエディキュラの中に人間が入る必要はなく，そばにいるだけでもよい。こうした，パターンと現実とのズレを埋める時にエディキュラよりももっと一般的な解としては，厚い壁でつくられた開口部や，何重にも構成された壁や，全体の構成，そして人々の動きを形づくる廊下などを挙げることができる。これらの解を導き出そうとするとき，そこに生まれる構成が，決して全体的なものにはならないように，即興性の発生する余地を残しておくようにしなければならない。生活行為が，そのパターンによって刺激を受けることはあっても，間違っても「心の宿る住まい」から逆に生活が細部まで支配されてしまうことのないように心がけなければならない。

MLTWは仕事を進めていくうちに，建築の古くから伝わっている要素を，敷地に合った，そこに展開する生活行為にふさわしい方法で使うことに興味を持つ

lish location in the house—to mark a place within, or at the outside, to which all parts of the house can be related; it sets, a measure for the place. The measure can be set in several ways, either as a central focus from which the rest of the house extends (as in the *Jobson* or *Johnson houses*), as an encompassing boundary that measures the house as a whole (as in the *Moore house* in New Haven, or the *Talbert house* in Oakland) or as an edge of special importance, either facing a larger space outside (as in the *Ottosen* and *Champy houses*) or joining a set of rooms along a passage (as in the *Rush* and *Stern houses*) or both (as in the *Hines house*). Often a combination of patterns is used to establish several scales of measure (the *Sea Ranch Condominium* or the *Moore house* in Orinda).

Each of these measures can be easily diagrammed—usually as a cluster of columns, a box, a pair of walls, or a colonnade. With the diagrammatic form established, the rest of the design process consists of working this archetypal form into the surrounding landscape, imaginatively inhabiting the space between. The use of the place is acted out, addressing the landscape on the one hand, and the measuring diagram on the other looking for places to sit or to squirrel away junk, gathering with friends, leaning against a column, resting on the edge of the outdoors; being behind, above, below, in front of and next to the elements of the building.

As the scheme unfolds new elements are added on—sheds, bays, porches that accommodate special needs or soften the edge between inside and out. Hollows will appear too—courts, niches and recesses carved into the building's form to carry light to a special place or create a sheltered cove outdoors.

Where walls are too confining, or block the light too much, they are regaled with window and door sized openings or dissolved into a truss. The resulting form of the house is like a narrative account of a dual struggle, between indoors and out, between idea and circumstance.

Sometimes the measuring scheme is so large that the action of the house is contained solely within, leaving pockets of space unclaimed. Sometimes, as with aedicules the measure is set so close that it serves as a focus —more to be next to than to be in. More usually the adjustment between archetype and reality takes place in thick edges, layers of space formed by walls or passages that serve both to organize the scheme and to accommodate specific acts, in each of these cases it is critical that the scheme not be total, that there be room for improvisation, for acting out a pattern of living that is informed by, but not controlled by the House of the Mind.

In the course of our work we have come to use most of the traditional elements of building in the process of relating an ordering scheme to its site and the activities within. Following are descriptions of those elements that we use singly and in combination to transform diagrams into buildings.

ようになった。以降，私たちがそれらを単独に，あるいは空間相互の関係を建築化するために他の要素と組み合わせて使う，そうした建築要素について解説することにする。

〈エディキュラ（小神殿）〉
そこに立ち上がって囲いをつくるもの――あるいは，その間隔に少なくとも人間の立てる空間をつくる一組の柱，あるいは，頭の上を覆うもの――これらは，古来，建築や絵画，そして文献に多く遺されてきたシンボリックな家に繰り返して使われてきたエレメントである。これら小さなエディキュラ神殿の内部には神々や英雄や，時には先祖が祀られている。エディキュラはある時はヒンドゥー教の神殿の外壁を覆い，他にも建築の多くの様式を形づくる大事な要素となってきた。エディキュラは家の重要な要素をミニチュアという形態で表現する。エディキュラはふつう4本柱や天蓋風の屋根を持っていて，家の中の象徴的な中心として機能することができ，一軒の家の中の，さらにその中に置かれた小さな家として特別な意味を持った場所をそこにつくり出す。エディキュラには生活するという行為に特別に必要な象徴的な意味が与えられている。またエディキュラは家の内部に展開する風景にランドマークを与える。そしてエディキュラが屋外に置かれた時には，その家に入るための儀式ばったエントランスとしての役割として，外から内への変換点を人々に象徴的に指し示す。

〈ベイ（小空間）〉
ベイは建物の中に小さく区分された空間であり，生活に貢献する面が大きい。ベイは建物の中に，そこに人々が入り込むのにちょうど適当な大きさの空間の単位をつくり出す。なかでもベイ・ウィンドウは，それが張り出している母体の部屋に対して，それから区切られた空間をつくり出すと同時に，それとひと続きの空間をもつくり出すという二重の意味を持っている。それはちょうど海に対してのベイ（湾）が陸に入り込むときに，そこに海の波濤が陸ともっとも容易になじめる場所をつくり出すように，ベイ・ウィンドウが屋外へ張り出す時には，そこに空間の雰囲気を保ちながら，しかも屋外に差し出されている感じを併せ持つ場所をつくり出すのである。ベイは座って陽の光を浴びる所であり，あるいは外を眺める所であり，あるいはそこに引っ込んだり，逆に人前で，そこに立ち現われたりする所である。ベイはそのスケールは小さいが，独立した建物そのものの性格をも反映することもできる。つまり，ベイはそれ自身外気にさしだされていて，屋根を持ち，あるいは，多くの場合，独立した，人の座るためのプラットフォームを中に持っている。ベイの3面にはふつう開口部がつくられ，時にはそれぞれの面に屋根まで付いていて，ベイに座っていると外で何が起こっているかを知ることができる。

ベイ・ウィンドウは外の眺めの良いところに設けられ，それが付くことによって部屋はその形の単調さを破って外に拡がり，家の外の表情に生活の意味のつくり出す襞をつくることができる。ベイがもっと大きくなると，今度はその家のメインルームとは分かれた，独立した空間をつくり出す役割を果すようになる。

〈キャノピー（天蓋）〉
キャノピーは，古来，帝王の権威を表わすシンボルであった。そこに帝王その人が座していなくても，ものとしてその権威を表わし，人々に丁重に扱われてきた。今日キャノピーは，大部分，中庭の日除けとして使われている。しかしずいぶん身をやつしたとはいえ，その持っている特別な場所を指し示す機能は古代帝王の玉座から今日の家の中にも転写されている。小さな空間の上に，その構造から独立した屋根が付けられたり，あるいは天井の中にさらにキャノピーが付けられたり，その部屋の中央高く，あるいは壁際に低くキャノピーのような形をした屋根を彫ったり描いたりすることによってそれはつくられる。一般に，キャ

Aedicules
Something to stand on, an enclosure—or at least posts to stand between—and a shaped cover overhead are the recurrent elements of symbolic houses represented in buildings, paintings and manuscripts. Such little aedicular shrines inhabited by gods, demi-gods and sometimes people, cover the surfaces of Hindu temples, and figure prominently in many styles of architecture. They state the essential elements of house in miniature form. Aedicules, often with four posts and a canopy can serve as symbolic focus for a house. As separate little houses within a house, they establish a very special place to be and they enshrine the act of inhabiting. Aedicules easily become landmarks in the internal landscape of a house. Placed on the outside they signify formal entry to the house, marking the place of transition from outside to in.

Bays
Bays, or compartments of buildings, are useful for being in. They establish for the building a unit of measurement that can be occupied, Bay windows are especially useful because they are both separate from and continuous with the room, they adjoin. Just as the bays of the sea penetrate the land and are places where the activities of the sea can most easily join the land, so do bay windows push into the outdoors and make places which can combine the qualities of being inside with exposure to the out of doors. Bays can be places to sit in the sun, to look out on the scene, to retreat into, or to appear in. Since they are small, they can reflect simple acts of building, with their own roof exposed, and often a separate platform to sit on. Since three sides can usually have openings and sometimes the roof can too, bays offer special chances to know what is happening outside.

Bay windows are located where special views or outlook are possible, or to allow a room to spread beyond the confines of its primary structure or to wrinkle the face of a house. Extra bays are also added sometimes to house special functions that are appropriately separated from the main rooms of a house.

Canopies
Canopies are an ancient emblem of royalty—symbolic of special care and attention even when royalty is absent. Now they are used mostly on patios. Yet their implication of specialness can be transferred to areas of the house, by providing a separate roof for a small space, by forming special canopies in the ceiling, or by revealing and painting a segment of roof that is shaped like a canopy, high in the center and lower at the edges. Generally, canopies are bright and colored.

Columns
Columns are something more than posts. Both are useful not only for holding up roofs but for marking a place to stand by. A column is a special event, a place where roof loads

ノピーには明るい色彩が施される。

〈コラム（円柱）〉
コラムは同じ柱ではあるが単なる柱（ポスト）とは趣が違う。両者とも，単に屋根を支えるだけではなく，そのそばに人々が寄って立つことのできる場所をつくり出すのであるが，コラムの方がより特別な意味を持っていて，屋根の荷重はコラムに沿って集中され，大地に伝えられるのである。だからコラムは，しばしば特別に扱われ，装飾されて，その重要性が表現された。コラムは背が高く，丸く太いほど，そしてそれが人間のサイズ以上に太い時に素晴らしい。コロネードは，コラム群が，一列になっていると感じさせるほど互いに近く立ち並んでいるもので，そこにつくり出されている空間が，何か公共のものであることを人に感じさせ，人々がそこに集い，あるいはある場所から他の場所へ移動していくためにつくられている。

〈ポーチ〉
ポーチは，それがエディキュラのようになっている場合でもあるいは他の場合でも，家を構成する最も重要なエレメントのひとつであり，まさしく，内部から外部への橋わたしを行うものである。そこには陽の光や雨は当たらないが，風はそこを通って行き，人々に外に開いた見晴しを与える。このように，屋根の付いたポーチは外と内との境目につくられ，その家に住んでいる人々は屋外で日光に当たってもよいし，覆いの下に入っていてもよい。ポーチによって家の外周全体が居住可能なスペースになると同時に，ランドスケープと室内がひと続きになる可能性がなくなり，採光が難しくなる。このようにして，家に接続するポーチはその母家の持っている可能性を拡大し，あるいはそこに境界線を引くことになる。エントランス・ポーチは，今日ではほとんど見られなくなってしまったけれども，家の私的な空間から通行の多い街路に面して張り出された私的な空間の前線でもある。もっとも今日では逆に，ポーチは公共の空間や陽の光からの，何か特別の外観を持った障壁のようなものとして考えられてしまう場合が多い。

〈屋根〉
屋根は，そもそもは建物に形を与えるものである（と言ってもそれが水平屋根でない限りにおいてであり，MLTWは水平屋根は使わない）。屋根の最も高い点と，低い点が定められると，屋根の勾配はその下に起こる諸々のことに厳しい法則を宣告する。つまり屋根の下り勾配の面で，壁の位置はどこまで前に出せるか，あるいは上の方の階はどこまで大きくとれるか，そして，それが屋根の下に納まろうとした時に，最上階はどこまで取れるか，というようなことについてである。中高の屋根は低い庇と，中心の頂点を持ち，そのピラミッドのような屋根はそれ自身完結したものであり，その屋根面に刻み目を入れたくなるようなものである。片流れの屋根は造作も単純で，ランドスケープや他の建築の形と関係すると最も素晴らしく見える。片流れの屋根は方向性をひとつしか持っていないため，片側は大変に高くなり，他方は大変に低くなる。この性格は，敷地が2方向から見るとそれぞれ異なっている時に有効である。MLTWは切妻屋根は使わない。入母屋はひどく威張りくさっているように思える。

屋根の形はできるだけ明快にすべきであり，天井が張られずにその構造材が露出される時には，その活発なありさまがその場を賑やかにする。傾斜屋根の屋根裏側も大事に扱わねばならない。それはつまるところ，大空の底を見上げているようなものなのだと言ってもよい。

つまりすべての家々は，どこかで大空の底に接しているのだ。屋根も大空と同じく，その下に暮らして心地良い。

〈階段，ステップ（段）とテラス（台）〉
階段は人々を大地から，建物のつくる高みへと導く。

have been gathered together and brought to the ground. Columns are often invested with special care and ornamentation that signifies their importance. They are best when they are big, round and fat, almost the size of people. Colonnades, with columns close enough together to form a series, imply that the place they form is somewhat public, specially formed for bringing people together or allowing passage from place to place.

Porches
Porches, aedicular or otherwise, are among the most helpful elements of a house, bridging, as they do, from inside to the out of doors. Sheltered from sun and rain yet open to wind and view, covered porches placed between outdoors and in offer the inhabitant a range of choice; to be exposed or sheltered or maybe some of each. Porches that ring a house make its entire periphery inhabitable but they also deny the possibility for immediate juxtaposition of landscape and room and make it difficult for sunlight to enter. Continuous porches limit, as well as extend, the possibilities of house. Entry porches can be, but seldom any longer are, places to hang out; private outposts along an active street. More frequently now porches are set for seclusion, away from public view and in the sun, with a special outlook if there is one.

Roofs
Roofs ultimately give shape to a house (unless they are flat, which ours seldom are). Once its highest or its lowest point is set, the slope of a roof sets rigorous limits on what can be done—how far forward the walls can be placed on the downward side, how large an upper floor can be, and where, if it is to fit under the roof with head room to spare. Hip roofs have low eaves and central focus, and their pyramidal forms are complete in themselves and thus good to carve into. Shed roofs are simple to build and look best when related to other landscapes or building forms. Since sheds slope in only one direction, one side is very high, the other quite low, which can be used to advantage when two aspects of a site are quite different. We seldom use gables. And gambrels are too bloated to consider.

Roofs can be built clearly and their structure, when revealed, can help to enliven the place with vicarious acts of building. The sloped underside of a roof is also an unmistakable form; it is, after all, the bottom of the sky.

All houses should somewhere reach to the sky. Roofs are good to be under too.

Stairs, Steps and Terraces
Stairs, steps and terraces reach from the ground into the heights of a building. As the land rises incrementally to become building, its shape is gradually transformed into the stepped increments that allow people to move easily up slopes. As these approach and enter the building, they are made of wood, stairs which can easily climb through the air to upper levels. The stairs of a house can deter-

大地が段々と高くなって建築へと姿を変える時，その形は階段状になって人々を登りやすくする。そして続いて建築の内部に入れば，そこは木でつくられていて，木の階段が空気の中を突き抜けて上の階へと通じて行く。家の中で階段は，人々の動きを決め，各部屋への入り方を決め，人々の通路を決め，人々の動きに振付けをする。階段は動きの起こる通路であり，休息をとる場所であり，下を見下ろす場所であり，しばしば，人々の進む方向を変える場所である。階段の一番下，ちょうど，広いプラットフォームから段々が分かれる辺りは，内部空間に設けられたテラス（台）のようなもので，人々はそこに座ることも，また，そこにものを飾ることもできる。階段が高くなればなるほど，それは急になり，上の階に登るという目的が強くなってくる。そして，とりわけ高い屋根裏部屋やプライベートな場所には梯子の方が望ましい。

〈ふつうの壁と大いなる壁〉
ふつうの壁は空間を分割し，大いなる壁は空間をひとつにまとめる。ふつうの壁は出入口を持っているが，大いなる壁は分厚く，その周囲にはとても住めない——少なくとも，そう見える。大いなる壁はそれ自身，家ほどに，いや家よりも大きい。それ故に，それはある大きさについての基準となり得る。大いなる壁は，時々小さな穴や窪みがあいている。それらは実際の出入口や窓よりも小さくて，私たちの身体は無理だとしても，心はそこに座ることができる。大いなる壁は，その壮大さによって，そしてその穿たれた開口部のパターンによって，過去の先達を思い起こさせる。そのほとんどはフランスとローマにあり，中国にはあまり見当らない。

ふつうの壁に付けられたドアや窓は多くの場合本物であり，その壁はその家のメイン・ルームの境界を形づくり，屋根や張り出しがそこから外につくられ，人々がそこに住むこともできる。あるいは，時には壁の中央辺りの位置に開口がとられ，下の方の開口は人の通路となり，上の方の開口には，素敵なオブジェが置かれて，その上のスカイライトから入ってくる光を浴びている。大いなる壁は，多くの部屋を結び合わせ，集中させて，ひとつのものにする。

ふつうの壁をどう扱ったらよいかということはだれでも知っている。その時，壁の材料の選択は大切である。——表面を荒くするか，平らにするか，明るくするか，材料の生地で仕上げとするか塗料を使うか，そして開口の位置もポイントとなる。

〈窓〉
窓は家に欠かせぬものである。窓は空間相互の関係づけをし，外観を決め，外と内との調整をする。大きな窓はそこから熱を逃がし，陽の光を導き入れ，人々にその恩恵を授けるべく配置され，さらに，日除けや，カーテンや，シャッターや，そういったものが取り付けられて陽の強さが調節される。

窓は，家の中に展開する生活を，最も饒舌に物語る要素である。平面や立面が推敲されるにつれ，窓やドアは人々の行為に位置を与え，その家の住人が，その街路に果たすべき役割を表わし，それを隣人がどう受け止めているかを人々に想像させる。それが開閉可能な窓ならば，そこからそよ風を迎え入れ，それと一緒に，（良かれ悪しかれ）物音や香りをも受け入れる。窓は水で洗うことを欠かしてはならない。

〈光：太陽の光，天窓，反射光，厚みのある光〉
光は，自然の運行していく規則を人々に最も身近に感じさせるものである。光は，天候の良し悪しや，季節の変化や，一日の中の時間によって変化していく。光はまた，相互に干渉し合い，壁面から壁面へ反射し，その様子を刻々と変える。光はダイナミックで生き生きとしており，それは建物それ自体は演ずることのできない素晴らしい性格である。いや，建物も光によって洗われている時は，その素晴らしさを演ずることができる，と言う方が正しいのかも知れない。MLTW

mine much of its action, regulating access to rooms, establishing paths and choreographing the movements of people. Stairs are designed as paths of movement, with places to rest and overlooks and often a change in direction. Their lowest levels, when spread into large platforms and steps, can be like terraces on the inside, places to sit or to set objects on display. The higher a stair rises the more steep and purposeful it is likely to become. For special high lofts or very private spaces, a ladder sometimes is in order.

Walls and Great Walls
Walls divide, great walls unify. Walls have openings. Great walls are thick and inhabitable—or appear to be so. Great walls are as big as, or bigger than, the house, so they naturally serve as a measure for it. They often have many openings and niches that are smaller than real doors and windows but large enough for the mind to occupy. Being big, and patterned with openings, great walls recall their antecedents, most of them in France and Rome, not China.

In some cases, the doors and windows are real and these walls are at the bounds of the main room of the house, with sheds and bays beyond them that people do inhabit. In other cases, usually at the center, the lower rank of openings serve for passage between rooms, while upper ranks lodge favored objects that greet the light as it enters through clerestories or skylights at the top. Great walls unify because they tie together many rooms, and focus attention.

Anyone knows how to use ordinary walls. The selection of material for walls is critical—rough or smooth, bright or dark, natural finishes or painted—and the location of openings is what gives them point.

Windows
Windows are what we design with. They open up relationships between spaces, establishing the outlook and the degrees of control between outside and in. Large windows lose heat, gain sun and provide an exposure which must either be desired and planned for, or subjected to a variety of controlling devices: shades, curtains, shutters and the like.

Windows are the most easily used narrative device, in acting out the life inside the house. As plans and elevations develop, windows and doors give position to activity and suggest what roles inhabitants will play and how publicly people assume them. Operable windows open to the breezes and their attendant sounds and smells, for good or ill. Windows also need washing.

Light: Sunlight, Skylight, Bounced Light, Thick Light
Light is the most ready evidence of the natural order. It fluctuates and changes with the weather and the season and the time. It is interactive, bouncing from surface to surface and changing its state as it does. Light is dynamic and alive, as nothing that we build

は，窓の配置をその壁と別の壁に近く設けるようにして，光がその壁に反射できるようにしたり，あるいは天窓を，太陽がその部屋を，日時計の文字盤のように横切っていくように取り付けたり，あるいは，その家の中心の場所が，思いも掛けぬ天窓の魔術によって光り輝くようにして，光の持つ素晴らしい可能性を実現しようとする。そしてそこでは，しばしば開口の壁の厚さが表現されているので，窓や天窓の隅がギラギラと照り返されるのでなく，むしろ明るく，柔らかに光っているように心掛けられた。家の隅の奥深い場が光に満ち満ちているときには，そこに座っているだけで無上の喜びが与えられる。

以上述べてきた建築の諸要素は，初めにもたらされたパターンを発展させ充実させるために使われる。MLTWは，それらの諸要素を一貫して増幅させるように努めてきた。そして，その建築が，その構成のされ方，その材料の選ばれ方，その中の人の動きの演出，大きなものと小さなものの並列，情景の多様性，そして，相互に重なり合ったパターンの面白さを実現しようと努めて来た。

　住宅の設計が進むにつれて，施主の情熱や，懐具合や，その地方の技術的特徴や気候や，そしてMLTWの仕事への根気が，デザインに大きな影響を及ぼす。MLTWは，あたかも「心の宿る住まい」それ自身がそうであるように多くの分身を持っている。ムーア，リンドン，ターンブル，ウィティカーの4人はプリンストン大学とカリフォルニア大学に揃って学び，教鞭を執った。その共有の体験をひとつにまとめて組織としたものであり，初めはバークレーに場所を構えた。後に，4人はそれぞれ違った場所に移った。チャールズ・ムーアはコネティカット州エセックスに，ドンリン・リンドンはマサチュセッツ州ケンブリッジに，ウィリアム・ターンブルはカリフォルニア州サンフランシスコに，そしてリチャード・ウィティカーはイリノイ州シカゴに移り住んだ。しかし今日でも，いくつかのプロジェクトにはMLTWは共同して力を合わせている。そして，MLTWは，それぞれの住む場所に，それぞれに事務所を構え，そして，それぞれの事務所にMLTWの仕事に欠かすことのできない所員がいる。とりわけ，マーヴィン・ブキャナン，ロバート・シンプソン，そしてウィリアム・グローバーの名前を落とす訳にはいかない。

　MLTWの建築は4人の手によって集団で設計され，その四つの意図や方法は，一つのものにまとめられている。4人はMLTWの共通のテーマを各人各様に解釈している。そして，4人共同で仕事をする時には，初めのテーマや構成を，より充実させ，発展させるべく討論する。MLTWの4人は離れた所にいるが，今も共通のテーマを，四つの異なった方法で推し進めている。ウィティカーとターンブルは，ランドスケープの中に，光の輝く通り路をつくりたいという願いからそれぞれに出発し，リンドンは，ランドスケープを見渡す小高い丘をテーマとして取り組み，そして最年長で，最も聡明なムーアは，現在，ロシアン・イースター・エッグ（何重にもなった層構成の代名詞）に凝っている。

1975年執筆
（和訳：石井和紘）

can be—except by being washed with light. We attempt to make the most of these qualities of light by placing windows and other openings close to walls and other surfaces that light can bounce off, or locating skylights so that spots of sun move across the room like shadows on a sundial, or so that the internal focus of a house glows with unexpected light. Often the openings are shaped to have thickness, so that the edges of the window or skylight are bright and soft, rather than harshly glaring. At the edge of a house thick places filled with light are good for sitting in.

These various elements of place are used to extend and elaborate the initial order. We work too, to develop them consistently, to have the place be suffused with a common spirit that can be discerned in the way things are built, the things they are made of, and in the pace of movement through the house, the juxtaposition of big and small, the possibilities for multiple views and overlapping patterns.

As a house develop, the specifics of its form are influenced by the client's passions and their purse, by local building practice and climate, as well as by our own continuing development. MLTW, like the House of the Mind, has many embodiments. Moore, Lyndon, Turnbull, Whitaker, first practiced together in Berkeley, as a firm that grew directly from experiences that we had shared studying or teaching together at Princeton and the University of California. Subsequently, we have settled in different cities; Charles Moore in Essex, Connecticut; Donlyn Lyndon in Cambridge, Massachusetts; William Turnbull in San Francisco, California and Richard Whitaker in Chicago, Illinois. For some projects, we still maintain collaborative practice. As we have worked in these several places, we have developed separate offices, and many others have contributed significantly to our work, most notably Marvin Buchanan, Robert Simpson, Robert Hayes, and William Grover.

Our work together as MLTW was formative for us all, consolidating the intentions and the approach that have continued to inform our work. Each of us interpret the common themes of MLTW differently. When working together, we each contribute to elaborating the initial scheme, inhabiting, extending and debating it. Separately we work with the same elements, each with a different bias: Whitaker and Turnbull are each in their own way likely to start with light filled passages through the landscape, Lyndon to work from high edges facing the landscape, Moore, oldest and wisest of the group, is inclined to Russian Easter eggs.

Written in 1975

Photographs are taken by Yukio Futagawa except as noted below.
pp.10-11, pp.14-15, pp.18-20, pp.26-29, p.33, p.37, pp.40-41, pp.43-48, pp.54-55, p.58, p.65, pp.70-71, p.72: photos by Yoshio Futagawa

'The Sea Ranch' by William Turnbull, Jr. was reprinted from "GA 3 The Sea Ranch" (A.D.A. EDITA Tokyo, 1971)
'The House of the Mind: Houses by MLTW' by Donlyn Lyndon was written for "Houses by MLTW" (A.D.A. EDITA Tokyo, 1975) and first published in this issue

ウィリアム・ターンブル著「シーランチ」は、『GA 3 シーランチ』(エーディーエー・エディタ・トーキョー発行, 1971年)より再録
ドンリン・リンドン著「心の宿る住まい：MLTWの住宅について」は、『MLTWの住宅』(エーディーエー・エディタ・トーキョー発行, 1975年)より再録。英文は初出

世界現代住宅全集 29
MLTW／ムーア, リンドン, ターンブル＆ウィテカー
シーランチ
コンドミニアム1／ムーンレイカー・レクリエーションセンター／オルソン・レクリエーションセンター
2019年10月25日発行
文：ウィリアム・ターンブル, ドンリン・リンドン
撮影：二川幸夫
編集・撮影：二川由夫
アート・ディレクション：細谷巖

印刷・製本：大日本印刷株式会社
制作・発行：エーディーエー・エディタ・トーキョー
151-0051　東京都渋谷区千駄ヶ谷3-12-14
TEL.(03)3403-1581(代)

禁無断転載

ISBN 978-4-87140-562-1 C1352